Boundless Theatre and Script Club present

T0353181

DRIP

**by Tom Wells (words)
& Matthew Robins (music)**

Drip was first performed on 1 November 2017 for Hull UK City of Culture for their Back to Ours programme, supported by Hull City Council. It was subsequently performed at the Paines Plough Roundabout as part of the 2018 Edinburgh Festival Fringe, the Bush Theatre and on tour.

DRIP

by Tom Wells (words)
& Matthew Robins (music)

Cast
LIAM   Andrew Finnigan

Words   Tom Wells
Music   Matthew Robins
Director   Jane Fallowfield
Designer   Russ Henry
Musical Director   Matthew Robins
Lighting Designer   Adam Foley
Stage Manager   Sarah Barton

Producer (Script Club)   Gabby Vautier

Production Supported by:

Arts Council England, Grants for the Arts
The Space
Hull City of Culture

Boundless Theatre and Script Club wish to thank:

The Shout Group at The Warren Project, Paul & Ruth
- Hull City Council Arts Team, Louise, Thom, Carys
& all at Back to Ours, Hull Truck, St Stephens
Neighbourhood Centre, Dales Youth Centre, National
Theatre Studio, Middle Child, Mike Bradwell,
Paines Plough, the Bush, Customs House Learning and
Participation team, Mosaic Youth Centre, Ros Terry,
Tom Stoppard, Nick Hytner, Richard Bean, Royal
Victoria Hall Foundation and Sir James Reckitt
Charity.

THE COMPANY

Andrew Finnigan | LIAM
Andrew trained with The Customs House, South Shields and the Theatre Royal Newcastle. Credits include: *The Fifteen Streets* (The Customs House, South Shields); *Scrapbook* (Live Theatre, Newcastle); *Broken Biscuits* (Live Theatre/Paines Plough and UK tour); *Drip* (Hull City of Culture/Back to Ours; *Wormtown*, *My Uncle Freddie* (The Customs House, South Shields).

Tom Wells | WORDS
Tom is from Kilnsea, East Yorkshire. Plays include: *Broken Biscuits* (Live Theatre/ Paines Plough and UK tour); *Folk* (Birmingham Rep/Hull Truck Theatre/Watford Palace Theatre); *Jumpers for Goalposts* (Paines Plough - Watford Palace Theatre and UK tour, 2013/14); *Cosmic* (Ros Terry/Root Theatre, E. Yorkshire tour, 2013); *The Kitchen Sink* (Bush Theatre, 2011, winner of the Most Promising Playwright - Critics Circle, 2011 and the 2012 George Devine Award); *Me, As A Penguin* (West Yorkshire Playhouse, 2009 and Arcola Theatre/UK tour, 2010) and *About A Goth* (Paines Plough/Òran Mór,2009). *Ben & Lump*, which Tom wrote as part of the Coming Up season (Touchpaper) was broadcast on Channel 4 in 2012 and his play *Jonesy* was broadcast on Radio 4. He has also written pantos for the Lyric Hammersmith and Middle Child, Hull. Tom is currently under commission to the Royal Court, the National Theatre and BBC Radio 4.

Matthew Robins | MUSIC/MUSICAL DIRECTOR
Matthew Robins is a multi-disciplinary artist and musician from the West Country whose work encompasses puppetry, film, music, sculpture, drawing, and performance. Matthew's work has been performed at venues including the Barbican, the National Theatre, Ulster Hall, the Howard Assembly Room, on the BBC, and at the London Film Festival, as well as making work for Tate Modern, Tate Britain and the V&A. A collection of Matthew's animations, songs, and interactive sculptures are on permanent display in the Science Museum, London.

As a film-maker, Matthew recently made a collection of stop-motion music videos for Passenger, as well as animations for Sivu, Fyfe and Led Bib, and has collaborated with Tori Amos (*The Light Princess*), and Phil Collins (*Tomorrow is Always Too Long*).

Matthew regularly tours with his band performing his own collection of home-made folklore - informed by his early years on the Cornish coast - his live shows combine puppetry, animation, songs, and storytelling.

Matthew's most recent work includes directing and designing an adaption of Ted Hughes' *The Iron Man* for the Unicorn Theatre in Southwark. You can visit sadlucy.com

Jane Fallowfield | DIRECTOR

Directing includes: *Red* by Somalia Seaton (Company 3); *Germ Free Adolescent* by Natalie Mitchell (Script Club Medway); *Bird* by Laura Lomas (Derby Theatre/tour); *Fingertips* by Suhayla El-Bushra (Clean Break); *Cosmic* and *Spacewang* by Tom Wells (Script Club Hull); *The Only Way is Chelsea's* by Frazer Flintham (York Theatre Royal/tour); *Lagan* by Stacey Gregg (Ovalhouse). Jane is Literary Associate at Talawa Theatre Company and previously Director on Attachment at Clean Break and Birmingham Rep (John Fernald Award). Other projects include co-running BBC London Voices, dance dramaturgy for Breakin Convention, sitting on panels and awards, and teaching at East 15 and Goldsmiths.

Russ Henry | DESIGNER

Russ Henry is the Managing Director of design studio and workshop Hot Soup House. Russ has worked on a number of high-profile events, creating bespoke set designs for festivals and theatre productions, and tailored furniture and fittings for offices, restaurants and bars.

Recent commissions include: *We're Still Here* (National Theatre Wales); The People's Platform for Common Wealth theatre; reclaimed office furniture for Filwood Green Business Park, Bristol; main stage for festivals Boardmasters and Love Saves The Day.

Adam Foley | LIGHTING DESIGNER

Adam trained at the University of Hull and is the Technical Director of Hull based company Silent Uproar. His theatrical credits include: *Small Wonders* (Punchdrunk Enrichment); *The Culture* and *Our Mutual Friend* (Hull Truck Theatre); *A Super Happy Story* (*About Feeling Super Sad*), *Pig* and *Small Plans* (Silent Uproar); *The Merry Wives* (Northern Broadsides); *Cinderella, Aladdin* and *Dick Whittington* (Middle Child); *Blackout* (Greyscale); *The Inappropriateness of Love, Freedom Books Flowers and the Moon, A Woman of No Importance… or Little Importance Anyhow* and *Tartuffe* (Paradigm Theatre).

Sarah Barton | STAGE MANAGER
Sarah is a production manager at Mountview
Academy of Theatre Arts where she has
managed several shows within their academic
season.

Recent credits include: *Lucky Stiff*,
Unnecessary Farce (Drayton Entertainment);
Mistatim (Red Sky Performance, Canadian/USA
tour); *Potted Potter* (Potted Productions,
Canadian tour); *L'elisir d'amore*, *Die
Fledermaus* (Toronto City Opera). This
winter, Sarah will be working with Scottish Youth Theatre
for their holiday production of *Tommy and the Snowbird.*

Gabby Vautier | PRODUCER
Gabby is a theatre and events producer for Echo Presents
and is co-director of Fertility Fest; the world's first
arts festival dedicated to modern families and the science
of making babies.

Gabby's current work for 2018-2019 includes: *Fertility Fest*
(Barbican); *Avalanche* (Barbican/Sydney Theatre Company);
Drip (Bush Theatre/UK tour); *SWIM* (HOME, Manchester) and
Macbeth (Secret Location).

Previous work includes: Head of Professional & Creative
Practice (Barbican/Guildhall); Creative Associate,
Directors Programme Producer and Audience Development
(Young Vic); Producer for *The Crash of the Elysium*
(Punchdrunk/Manchester International Festival); *The Quiet
House* (Birmingham Rep/Park Theatre London); *American
Justice* (Arts Theatre); Sound&Fury's *Kursk*, *Sus* and *Electra*
(all Young Vic)

Gabby is the mum of IVF twins and has seriously learnt to
multi-task! www.fertilityfest.com www.echopresents.com

WE ARE BOUNDLESS THEATRE

Boundless Theatre creates exhilarating, relevant and shareable theatre with and for young people and curious others. Our work responds to a vibrant and diverse global culture. We empower, inspire and invest in future audiences and artists now and promote conversation and exchange across the UK, Europe and internationally.

> 'An intriguing and surprising insight into millennial angst, *Natives* inspires sympathy for a generation that's wrongly perceived as invincible' **** (*Time Out*)

Boundless Theatre has toured over 25 productions across the UK and Europe. Productions have won critical acclaim and have been nominated for numerous awards (Stage Award, TMA Award, Herald Angel Award, Time Out Critic's Choice). Boundless Theatre provides a strong connection to Europe for artists, young people and audiences. It is about to embark on leading its third Creative Europe funded project, Extended Universe which will see the company collaborate with 3 new European theatres to co-create a large transmedia project from 2018-2020. Previous European projects have enabled the translation of over 90 of the best new plays for young audiences, and collaboration with artists, audiences and arts organisations from 22 countries.

Founded in 2001, the company (formerly Company of Angels) plays a key part in pushing the boundaries of theatre for young audiences through award-winning work across the UK and internationally. Under Rob Drummer's Artistic Direction, Boundless Theatre continues to produce the highest quality new theatre, and empower artists to be extraordinary

> 'It's the best play I've seen this year to articulate an urgent contemporary moment.' **** (*Metro* on *Natives*, 2017)

We believe that young people will change the world for the better and with encouragement, this change can be felt in the theatre that is made with, by and for them.

> 'I think what others think about teenagers and how to attract them in theatres, is by doing a play on gang lives and personally, that would not make me want to see it. But that's why I have started to like what Boundless Theatre is doing; they are taking a different approach on the things that interest us as teenagers'
> (Ange Marcel-Kassi, Year 12 student, Boundless Audience Member)

boundlesstheatre.org.uk

@boundlessabound

BOUNDLESS TEAM

Artistic Director (Joint CEO)	Rob Drummer
Executive Producer (Joint CEO)	Zoë Lally
Producer	Kirsten Peters Roebuck
Digital Producer	Debora Katia Tutta
Finance Manager	Mark Sands
Boundless Associates	James Frewer
	Rosie Elnile
	Elayce Ismail

BOUNDLESS BOARD

Charles Glanville (Chair)
Michelle Matherson
Claire Dikecoglu
Simon Gomes
David Beardmore
Spencer Simmons
Rachel Merriman
Sam Zdzieblo

BOUNDLESS ADVISORY GROUP

We want to make relevant work that enables 15-25-year-olds to see theatre as a vital part of their cultural experience. To keep us in check and to ensure we are being provoked to be ambitious with our plans we have an Advisory Group made up of brilliant young people who are drawn from different backgrounds: from theatre to parkour. Our Advisers meet with us regularly to see plays, talk big ideas, attend events and discuss what excites them most about being young today.

Robert Awosusi
Maya McFarlane
Finlay Ross Russell
Simon Marshall

Andrea Ortiz
Costanza Bizzarri
Andy McCredie

undless boundles
undless theatre the

BOUNDLESS SUPPORT: CREATE THE FUTURE NOW!

Raising aspirations, employability and inspiring creative expression for those facing visible and invisible barriers to the arts. Empowering more young people to network, develop skills and create, we will unlock soft-skills for future employment. Last year we supported 885 young people through UK projects, engaged 245 young people in European projects and gave 13 professional opportunities. With your support we can have an even greater reach and impact. Philanthropic support from individuals and trusts & foundations is vital to the future of Boundless Theatre. We just can't do it without you. For more ways to give please visit: **https://boundlesstheatre.org.uk/support/donate/**

BOUNDLESS ENTHUSIASTS

For those of you that believe as we do that every young person deserves the opportunity to be inspired by the highest quality theatre, we welcome your enthusiasm and support! The most valuable way of receiving support is through regular monthly donations. This means we can plan ahead and take more risks with our work, finding new ways to engage and empower young audiences, participants and artists.

'I enjoyed it because it was one of the first times in my life one of my ideas got listened to' (Year 9 Boundless Workshop Participant, City Academy, 2017)

BOUNDLESS FUNDERS

We are currently supported by Arts Council England as a National Portfolio Organisation. We are grateful for the support of The Space for Drip Digital.

Boundless Dialogue is funded by the European Union (Erasmus +). Extended Universe is co-funded by the Creative Europe programme of the European Union. We are grateful for the support of Arts Forward.

Anglo-Swedish Literary Foundation
Austrian Cultural Forum
Awards for All
Bourne Trust
Children's Forum Ltd
City of Quebec
Coutts & Co
Clore Duffield Foundation
D'Oyly Carte Charitable Trust
Ernest Cook Trust
Esmee Fairbairn Foundation
Education, Audiovisual & Culture
Executive Agency
EU Creative Europe
Cultural Commission
EU Culture 2000 Programme
Foyle Foundation
Garfield Weston Foundation
Goethe-Institut

Help a London Child
Hillingdon Community Trust
Kent County Council
Lloyds TSB Foundation
Mercers Company
Moose Foundation
Nederlands Instituut
Network for Social Change
Paul Hamlyn Foundation
Peter Minet Trust
Pro Helvetia
Redhill Trust
Romanian Cultural Institute
Royal Netherlands Embassy
Royal Victoria Hall Foundation
Southwark Theatres Education
Partnership
Swedish Embassy
Wates Foundation

'Boundless have been absolutely fantastic in their support… they've inspired me to create the most dynamic work and to place young people at the heart of my writing' (Glenn Waldron, Writer, *Natives*)

Boundless Theatre is a registered charity no. 1089185

Script Club

Script Club is a project that takes a writer into their local community to create a new play. We make new writing feel close to home by running workshops for young people with a writer that grew up nearby, sounds like them and shares experiences and local knowledge with them.

We take the play on tour, from local pop-ups in the community spaces where we run workshops, to studio spaces across the UK, taking our local story nationwide.

We have run 3 Script Clubs: *Cosmic* by Tom Wells (Hull), *Germ Free Adolescent* by Natalie Mitchell (Medway) and our first musical, *Drip* by Tom Wells and Matthew Robins (Hull). Previously as Root Theatre, we have produced *Bird* by Laura Lomas, *The Only Way is Chelsea's* by Frazer Flintham and *Lagan* by Stacey Gregg.

Our current production *Drip* was developed in collaboration with youth groups in Hull including LGBTQI young people at the Warren Project and supported by Arts Council England, Hull City Council and Hull 2017, where it received its premiere with the pop-up touring network, Back to Ours. It toured to Edinburgh Festival (Paines Plough Roundabout), the Bush Theatre and will embark on a national tour in 2019.

Script Club has received Arts Council England funding to develop two new projects in 2019/20, taking two new writers back into their local communities to create new plays.

If you'd like to learn more about the company, our future plans, and how you can support us, please visit **www.roottheatre.co.uk**

Script Club is led by director Jane Fallowfield.

Bush
Theatre
We make theatre
for London. Now.

The Bush is a world-famous home for new plays and an internationally renowned champion of playwrights. We discover, nurture and produce the best new writers from the widest range of backgrounds from our home in a distinctive corner of west London.

The Bush has won over 100 awards and developed an enviable reputation for touring its acclaimed productions nationally and internationally.

We are excited by exceptional new voices, stories and perspectives – particularly those with contemporary bite which reflect the vibrancy of British culture now.

Located in the newly renovated old library on Uxbridge Road in the heart of Shepherd's Bush, the theatre houses two performance spaces, a rehearsal room and the lively Library Bar.

bushtheatre.co.uk

Bush Theatre

THANK YOU

The Bush Theatre would like to thank all its supporters whose valuable contributions have helped us to create a platform for our future and to promote the highest quality new writing, develop the next generation of creative talent, lead innovative community engagement work and champion diversity.

LONE STAR

Gianni Alen-Buckley
Michael Alen-Buckley
Rafael & Anne-Helene Biosse Duplan
Garvin & Steffanie Brown
Alice Findlay
Charles Holloway
Miles Morland

HANDFUL OF STARS

Dawn & Gary Baker
Martin Bartle
Charlie Bigham
Judy Bollinger
Clive & Helena Butler
Grace Chan
Clare & Chris Clark
Clyde Cooper
Sue Fletcher
Richard & Jane Gordon
Priscilla John
Simon & Katherine Johnson
Philippa Seal & Philip Jones QC
Joanna Kennedy
V&F Lukey
Robert Ledger & Sally Mousdale
Georgia Oetker
Philip & Biddy Percival
Clare Rich
Joana & Henrik Schliemann
Lesley Hill & Russ Shaw
Team Nelson
van Tulleken Family
and one anonymous donor.

RISING STARS

ACT IV
Nicholas Alt
Mark Bentley
David Brooks
Catharine Browne
Matthew Byam Shaw
Tim & Andrea Clark
Sarah Clarke
Claude & Susie Cochin de Billy
Lois Cox
Susie Cuff
Matthew Cushen
Philippa Dolphin
John Fraser
Jack Gordon & Kate Lacy
Hugh & Sarah Grootenhuis
Jessica Ground
Thea Guest
Patrick Harrison
Ann & Ravi Joseph

RISING STARS (continued)

Davina & Malcolm Judelson
Miggy Littlejohns
Isabella Macpherson
Liz & Luke Mayhew
Michael McCoy
Judith Mellor
Caro Millington
Mark & Anne Paterson
Pippa Prain
Barbara Prideaux
Emily Reeve
Renske & Marion
Sarah Richards
Julien Riddick
Susie Saville Sneath
Saleem & Alexandra Siddiqi
Brian Smith
Peter Tausig
Guy Vincent & Sarah Mitchell
Trish Wadley
Amanda Waggott
Alison Winter
and three anonymous donors.

SPONSORS & SUPPORTERS

AKA
Alen-Buckley LLP
Gianni & Michael Alen-Buckley
Jeremy Attard Manche
Bill & Judy Bollinger
Edward Bonham Carter
Martin Bowley
Duke & Duchess of Buccleuch
The Hon Mrs Louise Burness
Sir Charles & Lady Isabella Burrell
Philip & Tita Byrne
CHK Charities Limited
Peppe & Quentin Ciardi
Joanna & Hadyn Cunningham
Leo & Grega Daly
Patrick & Mairead Flaherty
Sue Fletcher
The Hon Sir Rocco Forte
The Hon Portia Forte
Mark Franklin
The Gatsby Charitable Foundation
The Right Hon Piers Gibson
Farid & Emille Gragour
Victoria Gray
John Gordon
Vivienne Guinness
Melanie Hall
The Headley Trust
Brian Heyworth
Lesley Hill & Russ Shaw

SPONSORS & SUPPORTERS (continued)

Michael Holland & Denise O'Donoghue
Graham & Amanda Hutton
James Gorst Architects Ltd.
Simon & Katherine Johnson
Tarek & Diala Khlat
Bernard Lambilliotte
Marion Lloyd
The Lord Forte Foundation
Peter & Bettina Mallinson
Mahoro Charitable Trust
James Christopher Miller
Mitsui Fodosan (U.K.) Ltd
Alfred Munkenbeck III
Nick Hern Books
Georgia Oetker
RAB Capital
Kevin Pakenham
Sir Howard Panter
Joanna Prior
Josie Rourke
Lady Susie Sainsbury
Barry Serjent
Tim & Catherine Score
Search Foundation
Richard Sharp
Susie Simkins
Edward Snape & Marilyn Eardley
Michael & Sarah Spencer
Stanhope PLC
Ross Turner
The Syder Foundation
van Tulleken Family
Johnny & Dione Verulam
Robert & Felicity Waley-Cohen
Elizabeth Wigoder
Phillip Wooller
Danny Wyler
and three anonymous donors.

TRUSTS AND FOUNDATIONS

The Andrew Lloyd Webber Foundation
The Boris Karloff Foundation
The Boshier-Hinton Foundation
The Bruce Wake Charitable Trust
The Chapman Charitable Trust
The City Bridge Trust
Cockayne—Grants for the Arts
The John S Cohen Foundation
The Daisy Trust
The Equity Charitable Trust
Eranda Rothschild Foundation
Esmée Fairbairn Foundation
Fidelio Charitable Trust

TRUSTS AND FOUNDATIONS (continued)

Foyle Foundation
Garfield Weston Foundation
Garrick Charitable Trust
The Harold Hyam Wingate Foundation
Hammersmith United Charities
Heritage of London Trust
The Idlewild Trust
John Lyon's Charity
The J Paul Getty Jnr Charitable Trust
The John Thaw Foundation
The Kirsten Scott Memorial Trust
The Leche Trust
The Leverhulme Trust
The London Community Foundation
Margaret Guido's Charitable Trust
The Martin Bowley Charitable Trust
The Monument Trust
The Noel Coward Foundation
Paul Hamlyn Foundation
Peter Wolff Foundation
Pilgrim Trust
The Royal Victoria Hall Foundation
The Theatres Trust
Viridor Credits
The Williams Charitable Trust
Western Riverside
Worshipful Company of Meccers
Environmental Fund
The Wolfson Foundation
and one anonymous donor.

CORPORATE SPONSORS AND MEMBERS

The Agency (London) Ltd
Dorsett Shepherds Bush
Drama Centre London
The Groucho Club
THE HOXTON
Westfield London

PUBLIC FUNDING

If you are interested in finding out how to be involved, please visit **bushtheatre.co.uk/support-us** or email **development@bushtheatre.co.uk** or call **020 8743 3584.**

DRIP

Words by Tom Wells

Music by Matthew Robins

For Jane and Drew
with love, thanks and
a last-minute glitter cannon

Note on Play

Song lyrics are in bold text.

Miss Barton is named after our brilliant stage manager. If you're doing your own production of *Drip*, please name this character after your own stage manager.

This text went to press before the end of rehearsals and so may differ slightly from the play as performed.

LIAM, *fifteen*.

He is trying to be a very optimistic person.

This is our presentation we've done – me and Caz (best-mate Caz) – for The Project Prize.
I'm presenting it now, in assembly, cos you have to.
Caz helped with making it, gave really good feedback and that.
And also, she inspired it actually.
Told me not to say that but, I have done. Boom.
Miss Barton's on lights, from the back.

LIAM *gives Miss Barton a thumbs-up.*

And I know it's not... Like us doing a project, actually putting time and energy into extra work over the holidays, handing it in at the start of Year 11, you probably think that isn't that cool.
Cos, it isn't.
Thing is: we're not fussed.
Cos, thing is: we are actually mavericks.
Like decent, interesting people, with proper thoughts and voices and that. Stuff to say.
Who knew?
And if the world needs anything at the moment, it's flipping, mavericks.
So this is our maverick presentation.
One last-ditch desperate go at winning The Project Prize for Caz (and also me, but mostly Caz) instead of being ignored, overlooked, missing out, like usual.
Stuff you should know:

LIAM *strums his guitar.*

Um. It's a musical.
Four more things:

He sings.

Song – 'Four Things (i)'

**One. You'll notice as we go along a bit
This project's just a thing that we have made up in my room.**

Don't expect much.

**Two. I haven't got the hang of the guitar yet
It's just a work-in-progress, I'll mess up all the chords.**

You know, like life.

**Three. The characters are all just real people
I haven't changed the names at all.**

**Four. We don't mind losing
Just thought we'd have a go.**

Reckon that's everything.

Guitar strum.

Scene One

My bedroom is:

there's my bed, it's blue, my duvet cover and that;

my bookcase, with books (sci-fi) and comics;

on the top shelf, a clock, which is ticky, and some superhero
action figures.

My favourite's Spider-Man, obvs.

Sometimes I just look at him like: wow.

Sometimes I ask him for advice, sort of imagine he's giving
me advice.

Like if I'm worried or something.

'It'll probably be fine,' he'll say, in my head.

I'm trying to be more of an optimist, so.

It's good advice.

This has been my bedroom for one year exactly, since I moved
to Hull.

My mam started going out with a man called Barry, Barry
from Hull.

It happens.

And after a bit they like fell in love properly, wanted to make
a go of it, so me and my mam moved here, moved in with Barry.

He's got like a job and that, a house, a Nissan.

I wasn't sure at first. About him, or anything really.

Just sat in my room, didn't say much, ate toast.

That's all I do really.

I'm doing it now, at the start of this.

Mam says not to worry. Says it's just my age.

Song – 'Action Figures'

I am at that weird age
Half of me is all grown up
But I've still got action figures on a shelf
Near my bed
I am at a weird stage
I don't really have a life
I just sit here writing little songs
Instead

I am at that weird age
All the stuff that should be easy
Isn't easy, it's been tough now
For a bit
I am at a weird stage
Half of me is scared, scared of being noticed
Just in case they notice
I'm shit

The other half of me is pretty good
Oh, the other half of me is full of hope
When half of me is struggling
The other half can cope
Fingers crossed
The other half can cope.

Doorbell.
This is actually quite a special moment.
I don't realise it, but my life is about to literally change forever.

Guitar strum.

Scene Two

'Alright Caz.'
It's Caz, best-mate Caz at the door.
I flipping love Caz.
She's fifteen, she's hilarious, she's got a Saturday job at Lush.
I go in for a hug, she dodges it. Classic Caz.
'Liam, I'll get to the point,' she says.
The thing I love about Caz, she gets to the point.
'What are you doing right now?'
Feel a bit on the spot. I can't say I've been writing a song, she'd
piss herself.
'Nowt,' I say.
'Nice one,' she says. 'You're coming with me.'

Guitar strum.

Scene Three

Miss Barton, let's get proud.

Rainbow lights.

LIAM *hands out Pride flags.*

Little flags. Little flags. Little flags.
And then, I am going to choose…

LIAM *picks out a hunky audience member.*

…you. Big responsibility. When I point at you, please can you
shake this wind chime a little bit?

LIAM *gives audience hunk a wind chime.*

Thank you.

LIAM *stands in the middle*.

Right. We are standing, me and Caz, in Queen Victoria Square, and it is rammed.

Everyone is chatty, grinning, covered in rainbows.

Rainbow face paint, rainbow flags – waving – a rainbow fire engine, just in case.

There's music and cheering and that, from the parade.

Should've said: there's a parade.

Partly the parade is people blowing whistles, waving banners, dancing, and partly the parade is people carrying home-made-looking models of lesbian, gay, bisexual and transgender icons. I know.

Lily Savage, Sue Perkins, a massive papier-mâché Gok Wan.

Caz wouldn't say what was happening all the way into town, just said it was a surprise.

Which, it definitely is.

There's an eight-foot statue of Sir Ian McKellen dressed as Gandalf, on a stick. Wasn't expecting that.

But also, it's meant to be Project Prize inspiration.

'I'm not sure we can pull this off,' I say. 'In assembly.'

That's the rules of The Project Prize – you have to do a presentation of your project, in assembly.

(*Quietly*.) Ta-dah.

'I don't mean a parade,' Caz frowns. 'I just mean, like a big fun thing. Tear a little hole in all the stuff you're used to, boring stuff. Fill it up with better stuff. Sequins.'

There is a lot of sequins.

I'm listening to her, agreeing and that, nodding, but I'm also looking across the other side of the parade.

Cos, I recognise someone.

(*Whispers to audience hunk*.) Tinkle.

Audience hunk tinkles the wind chimes.

This lad from school. Year above, so he's just left actually.

Josh, I think he's called.

He's one of those people, he doesn't know you but he still holds doors open for you if you've got your hands full. One of those.

Start worrying he'll see us here, me and Caz, so I look away dead quick, hunch down a bit.

Then I realise he's also here, so he can't exactly judge.
Also, me and Caz are both fully out, like openly, hundred per
cent, it shouldn't be a surprise.
By the time I look up he's gone.
Caz is grinning. Properly beaming. I follow her gaze.
There's these two lads in the parade, properly fit, biceps,
shoulders, everything, they're wearing tiny swimming trunks,
nothing else, and they're carrying this massive banner of
Olympic bronze medal-winning diver Tom Daley. All round
him is gold, he's got wings. Everything about it is just: swoon.
Caz is enjoying it for different reasons.
'That's it,' she says. 'I know what we can do.'
Only Caz could be thinking about The Project Prize at a time
like this.

Guitar strum.

Scene Four

Backstory:
Caz has entered The Project Prize every year for the whole of
secondary school.
She's always up against Alex Mason, she always loses.
Cos Caz does good projects but like, they're not flashy, they
maybe don't stand out as much as Alex's.
Also, Alex's dad is Head of Governors. That's just how it works.
Which is a shame, cos he'd probably win anyway.
Even Caz says that.
I only moved here last year, Year 10, but she does talk about it
quite a lot.
Projects so far:

He sings.

Song – 'Four Things (ii)'

Caz learnt seven local bus timetables off by heart
And stood in the station in case people wanted help

Alex learnt Russian.

Caz dressed as an apple and did a sponsored silence
She raised twenty-three pounds for Guide Dogs for the Blind

Alex wrote a dystopian novel.

Caz helped her elderly neighbours with their gardens
Alex trained as a pastry chef

Caz re-creosoted the Scout hut
Alex did an internship at NASA.

We're back at mine now.
We're in my room, we're drinking squash, Caz is telling me her plan.
'It's already better than other years,' she says.
For a start, it's a team effort – me and Caz are in this together.
And we both fit under the umbrella term 'queer', which Caz reckons might help.
'Basically,' she says, 'we tick a box.'
Whatever Alex Mason does, he won't do that.
'It is all sounding really good,' I say. 'But, what is the actual project?'
'I want it to be a surprise,' she says. 'Meet me at Bev Road Baths, eight o'clock tomorrow. Tell you then.'
'But,' I say.
She shushes me.
'Just need your swimming shorts, a towel, and a can-do attitude.'
'Thing is – ' I say.
'I'm relying on you Liam.' Looks properly serious. 'Don't let me down.'
And then she just goes home.

Guitar strum.

Scene Five

I am looking at the poster Caz has made.
She's putting it up on the noticeboard next to the other ones, for
swimming lessons, lifeguard training, aquarobics. She hasn't
asked permission, so I'm keeping watch and all.
Nobody's fussed.
The woman behind reception's eating a massive pain au
chocolat and texting.
'Come and be part of Bev Road Baths' First Ever Synchronised
Swimming Team!' the poster says.
Then underneath there's some glitter glue, Caz's email address,
and what looks like a pirouetting dolphin.
Ambitious.
'You're my first teammate,' Caz says. 'What d'you reckon?'
'Oh,' I say.
'We'll do the first ever performance at the End of Summer Pool
Party,' Caz says, 'and film it to show in assembly.'
She says it like it's the obvious thing for us both to be doing.
'Though I'd better clear that bit with Steve,' she says.
I don't even know who Steve is.
But there's plenty to think about already, and I feel a bit panicky
to be honest.
Cos, here's the thing. The bombshell sort of thing.
I actually. I can't swim.
Everyone else learnt at school, in Year 3, but I had to sit it out.
I had grommets.
Caz is frowning. 'What is going on with you today?'
I think: better just do it, come clean, tell her.
But then, while I'm thinking, something else happens.
(*Whispers to audience hunk.*) Tinkle.

Audience hunk tinkles the wind chimes.

A lad slips past us in the porch bit, goes to reception, gives the
woman there his Tonic card.
'Hiya Josh,' the receptionist says.
Wafts her pastry at him.
He smiles, wanders off through the big door towards the pool.
I watch him go.

'Liam,' Caz says. 'You were telling me what's up?'
'Oh,' I say. 'Nowt.'
Caz grins.
'Ace. Let's flipping, do this.'

Guitar strum.

Scene Six

Right Year 11, remember I handed you a blue poncho at the
start, please could you all pop them on now? In this scene,
you're playing the part of: swimming pool.

Everyone gets their ponchos on.

There's little cubicles at the side of the pool, for getting
changed in.
I go in, sit down, try not to freak out.
My mam's always saying, the best thing to do with new things
is just chuck yourself in at the deep end.
Changing schools, meeting people, learning guitar chords.
Chuck yourself in at the deep end, she says.
I lock the door to my little cubicle, hope for the best.

LIAM *sings.*

Song – 'It'll Probably Be Fine'

The cubicle is cleanish
Not too puddly or hairy
It smells a bit of bleach
I always thought my swimming shorts were orange
But they're not
They're peach

I'm probably making something out of nothing
Trying not to whine
I can probably just swim just like instinctively
It'll probably be fine

I bag up all my clothes
Ram them in a locker
The towel's all unrolled
There's a sign telling you to have a shower
So I do
And it's cold

I'm probably making something out of nothing
Trying not to whine
I can probably just swim just like instinctively
It'll probably be fine

Stand at the edge of the pool
Deep breath knee bend
Ready to chuck myself in
At the deep end

I'm thinking about
Verrucas a lot
The chlorine smells quite strong
Everyone is splashing
Having fun but
I feel wrong

I'm probably making something out of nothing
Trying not to whine
I can probably just swim just like instinctively

And then I just:

LIAM *gets a mouthful of water, and jumps.*

(*Gurgling.*) **It'll probably be fine.**

Guitar strum.

Scene Seven

Quite a lot is happening at once.

LIAM *finds a trustworthy-looking audience member.*

Please can you look after this for me?

He gives them his guitar for a bit.

And if you wouldn't mind blowing these bubbles, symbolising underwater?

LIAM *gives out bubbles.*

And maybe some of you can spray me a bit with these? Just properly go for it. Okay? Ace.

LIAM *gives out water pistols.*

At the other end of the pool, Caz is chatting to the lifeguard.
He's probably Steve, I reckon.
She'll be sorting out our first ever performance, at the End of Summer Pool Party.
Steve's sat on his special high-up chair, nodding sort of vaguely, hoping she'll go away.
She's not leaving till he agrees.
So that's happening by the shallow end.
I know this cos there's a few times – maybe two or three times – I manage to get my head above the water, take a big, desperate breath, and I can see them chatting, before I splash and flail a bit and go underneath again.
They haven't noticed me. I wish they would.
Keep thinking: not like this.
Struggle a bit. Sink a bit.
Worry about Caz, how she'll feel.
Struggle a bit more. Sink a bit more.
I mean, The Project Prize is important, obvs, but maybe not this important.
And my poor mam, and Barry, who bought my shorts.
Hit the very bottom of the pool.
It's just me and this old, forgotten Elastoplast.
Realise: this is it.

Then someone with goggles on spots me, and stuff starts looking up.

A moment.

Now might be a good time to de-poncho, if you like.

Guitar strum.

Scene Eight

Caz is flipping livid.
'Right I'm not being funny Liam but you could've mentioned you can't effing' (I'm beeping out the rude words, for assembly, but you can probably still guess them. This one begins with 'F'.) 'You could've mentioned you can't effing swim.'
Me and Caz are poolside.
I just stand there and drip.
'Thank eff for...'
Caz points at –
'Josh,' he says.
(*Whispers, to audience hunk.*) Tinkle.
'Thank effing eff for Josh,' she says. 'That's all I'm saying.'
'Yeah, cheers,' I say.
He shrugs like 'no biggie'.
If I'd just saved someone's life and it was still technically breakfast time I'd be feeling pretty chuffed, but he's just acting like it's normal.
'What the effing eff were you thinking?'
Caz looks at me, fuming.
I shrug.
Josh smiles.
It's fair enough. Now I've stopped dying it does seem funny – there's a six-year-old on an inflatable Nemo who looks like we've made his day.

Caz brings the focus back to how I've really let her down. Like, really.

'Dunno what we'll do now,' she says.

Josh looks intrigued: 'What d'you mean?'

'Oh, it's nothing, it's fine,' I say.

'Oh it's fine is it?' Caz says. 'I mean I've put a poster up for Bev Road Bath's First Ever Synchronised Swimming Team, I've put my email on, I've committed to doing it for The Project Prize, which is actually the only good thing I've got going for me at the moment, my dad's being an absolute' (you fill that bit in) 'I've got that useless Tee double-yoo eh tee' – (she nods towards Steve the lifeguard) 'to promise we can do our first routine, first proper public performance at the End of Summer Pool Party in like three weeks – '

'Cool,' Josh says.

'Trouble is,' Caz carries on, 'the only person I've got on my synchronised swimming team, apart from me, obvs, is Liam. And he can't swim.'

Josh smiles. Looks at me. 'I'll teach you.'

'Oh,' I say. 'It's fine, you don't have to…'

'Shut up Liam,' Caz says, with her eyes.

Josh looks a bit awkward.

'That's what I'm hoping to do like all the time, eventually.' he says. 'Teach people how to, teach swimming lessons.'

Caz looks at him a bit doubtful.

'I'm like, nearly a lifeguard,' he says. 'Course starts Monday.'

Caz looks a bit less doubtful. Not exactly impressed, but still. And I just look at him like. Well, I dunno.

Song – 'You're Not A Lifeguard (But You Will Be Soon)'

You're not a lifeguard but you rescued me
You're laughing like it wasn't a big deal
You're not a lifeguard but you will be soon oh oh
You're starting the course next week

You're not a lifeguard but you saved my life
The actual lifeguard didn't see
You're not a lifeguard but you've got all the skills oh oh
You're sort of a lifeguard to me

And you've got shoulders and arms and a smile
That's a little bit wonky

But still lush
And I'm stood here by the shallow-end sign
Trying
Not to blush. And blush. And blush.

Realise I'm just like gazing at Josh, for no reason.
Caz swoops in.
'If you're teaching him to swim,' Caz says, 'can I also interest
you in joining Bev Road Baths' First Ever Synchronised
Swimming Team? It'll be immense.'
Josh smiles.
'No thanks,' he says, friendly as. Caz looks like: fair enough.
Wish I'd just done that.

Guitar strum.

Scene Nine

Caz is round mine all the time.
There's better biscuits here, she says, and her dad's doing her
head in.
He's hard work, Caz's dad. Drinks too much then gets quite sad.
And we do have good biscuits.
Mostly Caz finds YouTube videos for us to watch, of the
Russian Olympic synchronised swimming team.
They're amazing.
March out like robots, with tons of make-up on, fixed smiles,
dive in, perfectly, start doing all these really complicated lifts
and patterns in the water, perfectly, like a kaleidoscope made
of people.
When they do something really spectacular, Caz nods, dead
serious, makes a note of it.
As if we will be able to do it in our routine.
Which, we definitely won't.

So far, there's only the two of us. And I can't swim.
Not properly. Not yet.
I am trying though, and Caz says I'm clearly making progress.
Sometimes she gets me to walk through potential routines on
dry land, or practise breast stroke on a stool.
I'm fairly good at that.
Actual swimming, not so much.
But lessons are fun.
Josh is genuinely quite a good teacher. He's calm and patient
and he smiles a lot.
Reckons there's four main rules for learning how to swim.

LIAM *sings*.

Song – 'Four Things (iii)'

One. Try and keep your head above the water
It's really doable when you've got armbands and a float.

Otherwise you'll drown.

Two. It's always that bit better to keep moving.
Your legs are quite dependable, just kick them if you can.

Otherwise, you'll drown.

Three. Keep your chest and tummy held up high.
(That's how Tom Daley got his abs).

Four. Try not to overthink it. Otherwise you'll drown.

To start with I have a float and armbands and he's all 'kick your
legs' and I do, and it's sort of fun, which is nice.
And then Josh is like: 'Think it's time for the noodle.'
The noodle's immense.
It's just like a massive noodle, if you can imagine that. But
instead of being made of noodle, it's made of foam, so it floats,
and you sort of tuck it here, under your arms, and then just
swim like everyone else. No armbands just:

LIAM *shows us, while hopping*.

Do three whole widths with the noodle and that is lesson one.
Lesson two's more noodle-work.
Comes quite easy now.

Noodle-wise, I'm a natural.

Lesson three starts off with Josh saying 'Shall we try it without the noodle?'

I'm not sure about that, but I do it, and I sink straight away, cough, swallow half the pool, get really annoyed with him, but it's really that I'm annoyed with myself, and I think probably we both realise this, but anyway, I go back to using the noodle again.

Then at the end we have another go, noodle-less, and I actually manage it.

Which feels: immense.

A whole width.

I do get overtaken by a five-year-old and she's not that gracious about it but I just think: fair enough, she's basically a mermaid.

We get out, get changed, get some celebratory chips.

Josh lives on the way back to mine so, nearly anyway, it's just like a tiny detour, so I sort of walk him back to his.

Dunno why, it's just nice.

Then I cock it up.

We're saying bye outside his front gate, and for some reason I just like hug him – I'm just naturally quite huggy, it's normally fine – but in this case I can tell it isn't fine.

He freezes, pre-hug.

I mean it's just a hug but. I let go really quick.

Feel bad. Go home.

A moment.

Might as well take this back.

LIAM *takes the wind chime back from the audience hunk.*

Guitar strum.

Scene Ten

Fast forward.
It is the night before the End of Summer Pool Party, we're in my room.
Caz is excited. I could vom.
She's talking me through the routine, like:
Circle, circle, underwater circle, pop up, freeze, blossom out like a flower. Twice.
It feels ambitious.
Josh got a bit busy with his lifeguard course for any more lessons or anything, so I've not seen him since Hug-gate, the Hug-gate Scandal.
Caz is spending more and more time round mine, cos her dad's in a bit of a state.
It's all adding up.
Harder and harder to feel optimistic.
I've turned Spider-Man round, he's facing the wall.
Caz hasn't noticed.
She must sense I'm worried though cos she does this big rallying speech.
Tells me she's proud of the team we've become.
Cos like the Olympic ones are graceful, yes, precise and that, poised, controlled, those are their strengths.
But we've got our own strength, Caz reckons.
Our strength is: enthusiasm.
To inspire us even more, she's nicked a load of bath bombs from work.
We do a couple in the sink, just to watch what happens.
They fizz, all different colours, blossom out. Shimmer a bit.
But I'm still not feeling it to be honest.
I've got quite a lot of worries.
In the end, Caz just like deals with them head-on.
'Tell me what you're worried about,' she says, 'I'll tell you why you're wrong.'
So I do:

Song – 'Dive Right In'

I'm worried. I'm really worried.
I'm slightly falling apart.

What if we're all ready but
I'm too scared to start?
Too scared to start

Then Caz goes:

Dive dive dive right in,
You just have to dive right in,
Dive dive dive dive dive right in
Dive right in
You just have to dive right in
Dive dive dive dive dive dive dive right in.

Then I go:

I'm worried. I'm really worried.
Not that good at swimming yet.
What if I get out there
And suddenly forget?
Suddenly forget

And Caz goes:

Swim swim swim like mad,
You just have to swim like mad
Swim swim swim swim swim like mad,
Swim like mad,
You just have to swim like mad
Swim swim swim swim swim swim swim like mad.

'See?' Caz says. 'It'll be fine.'
I don't say anything.
'Please Liam.'
Wasn't expecting Caz to say please.
Don't know what to do.
Look at Spider-Man.
He's still facing the wall though, obvs.

I'm worried. I'm really worried
We both know we are shit.
What if we spend the rest of school
Regretting it?
Regretting it

Make make make a splash,
You just have to make a splash

Make make make make make a splash
Make a splash
You just have to make a splash
Make make make make make make make a splash
Make make make make make make make a splash.

Guitar strum.

Scene Eleven

Just got to distribute some pool party paraphernalia.
Beach balls.

LIAM *hands out some beach balls.*

Garlands.

LIAM *gives out some garlands.*

That sort of thing.

LIAM *starts inflating a small dolphin.*

Me and Caz go into cubicles next to each other, get changed.
It's quite old-school just having cubicles at the side of the pool,
but Bev Road Baths is, all twisted cast-iron swirls on the
balcony, massive windows in the roof. The way it's been done
up tonight just adds to it. Lights, bunting, inflatable fish.

LIAM *hands the dolphin to an audience member.*

The pool party is already in full swing. There's loads of people
from school just having a laugh, wearing swimsuits, bikinis,
saying cool stuff like 'hey' – that sort of thing. Some sort of
sound system's playing Ed Sheeran. Exactly.
Strip off down to my peach shorts, which I had on underneath
anyway, put my socks and that into my bag.

The music changes, to Sia.

She's quite dramatic isn't she?

Think that's maybe why, out of nowhere, I suddenly have this like massive revelation.

Like life-changing, earth-shattering, mind-blowing, all that.

Sit on the little bench, and I just know: I can't do it.

I can't go out there in front of all these people from school, confident people, who just fit in, without even trying, I can't go out there and doggy-paddle my way through an underwhelming synchronised swimming routine with Caz.

I just can't.

Cos even if we do it better than we've ever done it before, which we won't, but even if we do, this lot'll still take the piss.

It won't be a bath bomb or a kaleidoscope.

It won't be a magic, sparkly rip in boring, ordinary life.

It'll be me and Caz, wet and pathetic, getting laughed at.

Then they'll put the disco back on.

'You ready Liam?'

Caz is stood outside my cubicle.

She sounds strong. Sure.

Maybe even adrenalin-y.

I don't know what to say.

'Liam?'

Just lift my feet up, so she can't see me any more, under the cubicle door. Sit cross-legged on the bench, like I'm meditating or something. Hope and hope and hope she'll go away.

Guitar strum.

Scene Twelve

Caz is still stood outside my cubicle. It's been about thirty
seconds.
I'm still not unlocking the door, I'm not even admitting I'm in
here, which is daft I know but it's what's happening.
'Liam!' Caz is properly cross. 'Get out here now.'
I don't move.
For ages.
Like, three songs.
And one of them's a medley.
I'll just skip ahead though, stop things dragging too much.
Caz gives up in the end.
Goes and tells Steve the lifeguard it's not happening.
I watch through this tiny gap between the door and the frame.
He shrugs like: 'Thought not.'
Everyone else just carries on partying.
They didn't know anything about it anyway.
Caz gets dressed again, goes outside, round the back, to wait for
her dad.
I don't like to think of her just stood there by herself, under that
overhang-y bit of roof, getting rained on.
But I reckon she probably is.
This is Caz's Sad Song. You just have to imagine I'm Caz for
a bit.

LIAM *sings*.

Song – 'Caz's Sad Song'

I like it a lot better in the car park
You don't have to pretend everything's ace
Overhear the lads taking the piss
And keep a massive smile on your face

My dad said he'd be here at eight
He's only twenty minutes late
It's fine to just stand under this and wait
And wait

They've really started cranking up the disco
They're playing Little Mix dead loud

I sort of wish I could be part of it
I sort of know I'm not really allowed

My dad said he'd be here at eight
He's only twenty minutes late
It's fine to just stand under this and wait
And wait

It's always raining in the car park
It always looks a lot more fun inside
But some of us are just built for the car park
Sometimes it is better just to hide

My dad said he'd be here at eight
He's only twenty minutes late
It's fine to just stand under this and wait
And wait.

Guitar strum.

Scene Thirteen

It's been three days and I've not spoken to anyone apart from
my mam, and someone who rang up about accidents or injuries
at work.
I keep thinking Caz'll ring and she'll have a new plan all ready.
She hasn't done.
And then, keep hoping I'll bump into Josh and all.
I can't face going for a swim though, which is the only way
really I'd bump into him.
Unless I hung about outside his house, which would be weird.
To try and stir things up a bit on social media I've put a little
photo of me buying some cigarettes.
I've been thinking about it a while actually, thinking maybe

that's a good way to get some new mates, just in case.
People who smoke. Or maybe vape.
Just waiting for everyone to see it and be like: 'Wow. You're smoking now, amazing.'
And I can be like 'Yeah.'
Although, I haven't actually started yet.
Apart from that it's just the usual really.

LIAM *sings*.

Song – 'I've Ruined Absolutely Everything'

Netflix, read, have a wank.
Try to smoke but it is rank.
Go downstairs
Mam's not back yet
Try another cigarette.

Make toast.
Check Facebook.
Nobody has liked my post.
Eat some toast then eat more toast.
(I love toast.)

I'll just say I was joking
About smoking.

Miss Barton, the capo's off.

Lonely
Miss my mates
Check my Facebook
No updates.

I've ruined absolutely everything
The one time Caz relied on me I really let her down

Josh never liked me in the first place
I just got full of hope cos he's a lad and he was nice

Spider-Man is just a toy.
Spider-Man is just a toy.
Spider-Man is just a toy.

LIAM *kicks Spider-Man over*.

A moment.

LIAM *looks at the mess he's made.*

Thought it might help a bit, to get it off my chest.
It hasn't.
Reckon I need to actually do something.

No guitar strum. LIAM *is too focused on the task at hand.*

Scene Fourteen

Knocking.
Josh answers, dead shifty, but I'm ready for it.
'Calippo?' I say. Offer him a lolly.
'Um. Okay?'
He's not sure what's going on.
'Walk?'
Here's what I'm thinking:
One: everyone loves a Calippo – fact – and:
Two: hopefully he'll be less weird if we're not right by his
house.
Reckon maybe he's still got some coming out to do.
Which is, you know. Completely fair enough.
He smiles.
'Go on then.'
Just like that: we're wandering.
He's telling me about his lifeguard course, which he passed,
obvs, so now he's got a job and stuff, and he's off to do some
shadowing of the swimming instructors so he can get started,
do the training for teaching swimming lessons, his number-one
dream.
And then I tell him about the Pool Party disaster, how Caz isn't
speaking to me and how I've basically shat on her dreams of ever
winning The Project Prize, which she definitely deserves to win.
How I wish I could make it better. And cos, I dunno, maybe cos
I've not had many people to chat to just lately, or maybe cos it's
just nice chatting to him, to Josh, start telling him about
everything – eating toast, trying to smoke, Spider-Man, writing
little songs, just like rubbish little songs, which I've never told

anyone before but. Ever but. But anyway. We sit on a bench in
Pearson Park, think things through a bit, things I could do to
make stuff better. He's got his arm round me, just without
realising it I think, or just cos it happens. Feels nice.
And it's Josh's idea really, the musical.

Guitar strum.

15.

Scene Fifteen

'This is the last bit of the presentation.'
I'm explaining it to Caz.
She pretended she wasn't in for ages, but then her dad bellowed
at us to stop making such a racket, which we weren't, we were
just knocking on the door, but Caz came downstairs in case he
got properly mad, said if we wanted to chat we should probably
do it somewhere else, so we all ended up back at mine.
Me and Caz and Josh.
Feels a bit weird having Josh in my room.
Like he's literally sat on my bed.
Which I have actually imagined a number of times.
Hopefully he can't tell.
I'm a bit embarrassed in case he notices Spider-Man.
He's mostly just looking at my guitar though.
I've sung them all my songs, all the ones I've written this
summer, which Josh says he really likes, and Caz says are pretty
basic but okay.
She's still angry. Says she isn't but I tell her I get it.
'Cos we never did the routine,' I say. 'Cos of me. But there's
still time to do something. Tear a little hole in all the stuff we're
used to, boring stuff. Fill it up with better stuff. Sequins.'
'You won't though will you?' Caz says.
'I will,' I say. 'Promise.'

And I show Caz all these ideas I've got, written down, for
the end.
She's starting to smile a bit.
Like maybe we might end up being mates again.
So: this is it.
The bit where I need a bit of help:
One: to do the last song all of us together.
Two: to seal the deal with me and Caz being best mates again.
The grand finale of this: our Project Prize entry.
Which is me doing the synchronised swimming routine that
never happened.
Apart from on dry land, in assembly.
Miss Barton – hit it.

Music plays.

It's bunting time.

LIAM *gets bunting out of his bag.*

If I give this to you, please can you hook it up there?
Thank you.

LIAM *picks up the microphone.*

Don't go anywhere. I'll be back in a sec.

Pause.

LIAM *goes offstage.*

(*Offstage.*) Excitement mounts.

Pause.

(*Offstage.*) The suspense is too much.

Pause.

LIAM *reappears, in his swimming shorts, with more things to
give out.*

Stuff to give out.
We've got: one big shark – for you…

He gives someone a shark.

A pineapple, for you.

He gives someone an inflatable pineapple.

We've got three noodles, for you three.

He gives the noodles out.

And, most importantly, we've got a song.
Here's the thing with the song.
I'll do the verses, just me. I'm on verse duty.
You lot join in for the choruses.
Just properly go for it.
And if you're feeling a bit shy about joining in, a bit awkward
or whatever, just remember: I'm stood here, in assembly,
wearing tiny peach shorts.
So I go:

LIAM *sings.*

Song – 'Dive Right In (Again)'

I'm worried. I'm really worried.
I'm slightly falling apart.
What if we're all ready but
I'm too scared to start?
Too scared to start.

Ready?

Dive dive dive right in
You just have to dive right in
Dive dive dive dive dive right in
Dive right in
You just have to dive right in
Dive dive dive dive dive dive dive right in.

That was immense.

I'm worried. I'm really worried.
Not that good at singing yet.
What if I get out there
And suddenly forget?
Suddenly forget.

Sing sing sing like mad,
You just have to sing like mad
Sing sing sing sing sing like mad

Sing like mad
You just have to sing like mad
Sing sing sing sing sing sing sing like mad.

I'm worried. I'm really worried
I might fall flat on my face
Or what if we make something
Accidentally ace?
Accidentally ace.

Make make make a splash,
You just have to make a splash
Make make make make make a splash
Make a splash
You just have to make a splash
Make make make make make make make a splash.

Synchronised swimming routine:

LIAM *does the synchronised swimming routine.*

Circle circle, underwater circle
Jellyfish, pop up, freeze
Blossom out like all the bath bombs
Caz nicked from Lush
Shimmer fizz

This this is the end
This this this this this is the end
This this really is the end
Is the end
Thank you for not taking the piss
Now would be the perfect time for clapping
Now would be the perfect time for clapping.

The End.

FOUR THINGS (i)

words by
TOM WELLS

music by
MATTHEW ROBINS

ACTION FIGURES

words by
TOM WELLS

music by
MATTHEW ROBINS

♩=175 bright and steady, with spirit

I am at____

that weird age   half of me___ is all grown up_____

but I've still_ got AC TION FIG-URES on a shelf   near

my   bed   I am at_____   a weird stage

_____ I don't rea - lly have a life____ I just sit here writ - ing

71 | D   C G   Em   Bm   Am
___ of me___ is pret - ty good___   oh - hhh   the ot - her

78 | D   Bm   C   G
half of ___ me_____ is full of hope. when half of me___ is strug

82 | Am   C   D   D(sus4)   D
gl - ling_ the ot - her half _ can cope___

87 | C   D   G C G
fin-gers crossed   the ot-her half _ can cope.

FOUR THINGS (ii)

words by
TOM WELLS

music by
MATTHEW ROBINS

steady

♩=180 (♩=♩)

Caz learnt se-ven lo-cal bus time tab-les off by heart and stood in the

sta-tion in case peo-ple wan-ted help Caz dressed

as an ap-ple and did a spon-sered si-lence she raised twen-ty three pounds for

guide dogs for the blind Caz helped her el-der-ly

neigh-bours with their gar-dens A-lex trained as a pas-try chef

Caz re - cre - o - so - ted the scout hut

A-lex did an in-tern-ship at NA-SA.

IT'LL PROBABLY BE FINE

words by
TOM WELLS

music by
MATTHEW ROBINS

one is splash-ing ha-ving fun but I feel wrong

I'm prob-ab-ly mak-ing some-thing out of no-thing

try-ing not to whi-i-i-i-i-ine I can prob-ab-ly just swim just like

in - stinc - tive - ly

it' - ll prob-ab-ly be fine

YOU'RE NOT A LIFEGUARD
(BUT YOU WILL BE SOON)

words by
TOM WELLS

music by
MATTHEW ROBINS

♩=120 lilting waltz

li - ife   Th-e ac-tu-al life - guard did-n't see

You're not a   life-guard but you've got all the skills   oh____   oh - oh-oh

ohh   you're sort of a   life- guard to   me   and you've got

shoul- ders___and arms and a smile___ that's a lit tle bit won-ky   but still lush and

I'm stood here by - y the shal-low end si - i - gn try-ing   not to blush

and blush   and____   blush

(whistle melody ad lib and drift off before reaching the end of the phrase)

FOUR THINGS (iii)

words by
TOM WELLS

music by
MATTHEW ROBINS

one, try and keep your head a-bove the wat-er it's real-ly do-a-

ble when you've got arm-bands and a float

two, it's al-ways that bit bet-ter to keep mo-ving your legs are quite de-

pen-da-ble just kick them if you can three,

keep your chest and tum-my held up h-igh that's' how Tom

Da-ley got his abs four, try not to o-ver

think it ot-her wise you'll drown.

DIVE RIGHT IN

words by
TOM WELLS

music by
MATTHEW ROBINS

CAZ'S SAD SONG

words by
TOM WELLS

music by
MATTHEW ROBINS

♩. = 66   gentle ballad

I like it___ a lot bet-ter___ in the car park_____

you don't have to pre-tend ev-ry-thing's ace   ov-er- hear_ the

lads tak-ing___the piss   and keep a mas-sive smi-le on___ your face._____

My dad said he'd be here at eight   he's   o-on-ly_____   twe-en-ty_____   min- utes___

late   It's fine to just stand un-der this_ and wait.   and wait.

They've rea-lly___ star-ted crank-ing___ up the dis-co_____   They're play_ ing

bet-ter just to hide_____ My dad said he'd be here at eight he's

o-on-ly_____ twe-en-ty_____ min utes____ late It's fine to just stand

un-der this____ and wait. and wait.

I'VE RUINED ABSOLUTELY EVERYTHING

words by
TOM WELLS

music by
MATTHEW ROBINS

DIVE RIGHT IN (AGAIN)

words by
TOM WELLS

music by
MATTHEW ROBINS

♩=170 steady but not too strict

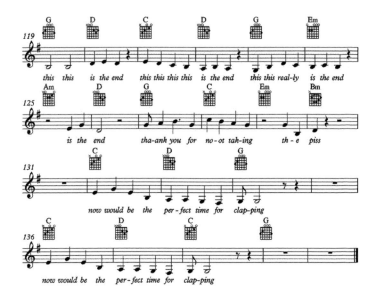

this this   is the end   this this this this   is the end   this this real-ly   is the end

is the end   tha-ank you for no-ot tak-ing th - e piss

now would be the per - fect time for clap-ping

now would be the per - fect time for clap-ping

A Nick Hern Book

Drip first published as a paperback original in Great Britain in 2018
by Nick Hern Books Limited, The Glasshouse, 49a Goldhawk Road, London
W12 8QP, in association with Script Club, Boundless Theatre, and the Bush
Theatre, London

Words copyright © 2018 Tom Wells
Music copyright © 2018 Matthew Robins

Tom Wells and Matthew Robins have asserted their right to be identified as the
authors of this work

Cover image by Matthew Robins

Designed and typeset by Nick Hern Books, London
Printed in the UK by Mimeo Ltd, Huntingdon, Cambridgeshire PE29 6XX

A CIP catalogue record for this book is available from the British Library

ISBN   978 1 84842 809 6

www.nickhernbooks.co.uk

facebook.com/nickhernbooks

twitter.com/nickhernbooks